# DENTISTS

## PEOPLE WHO CARE FOR OUR HEALTH

Robert James

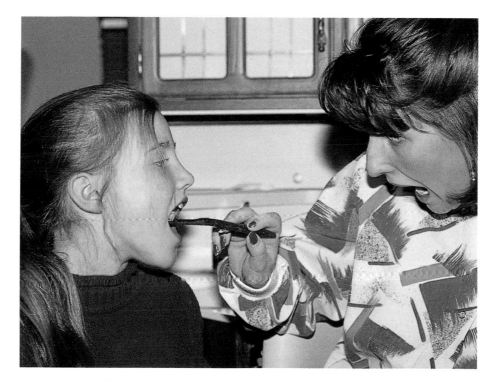

The Rourke Book Co., Inc.
Vero Beach, Florida 32964

Acknowledgments:
The author thanks Dr. Gary Ahasic and his staff for their help in
preparing photos for this book

**Library of Congress Cataloging-in-Publication Data**

James, Robert, 1942-
   Dentists / by Robert James.
     p. cm. — (People who care for our health)
   Includes index.
   Summary: Describes what dentists do, where they work, and
how they train and prepare for their jobs.
   ISBN 1-55916-169-8
   1. Dentistry—Vocational guidance—Juvenile literature.
[1. Dentistry—Vocational guidance.  2. Occupations.
3. Vocational guidance]
I. Title  II. Series: James, Robert, 1942-  People who care for our
health
RK63.J34  1995
617'.6'023—dc20                    95–18942
                                     CIP
                                     AC

**Printed in the USA**

# TABLE OF CONTENTS

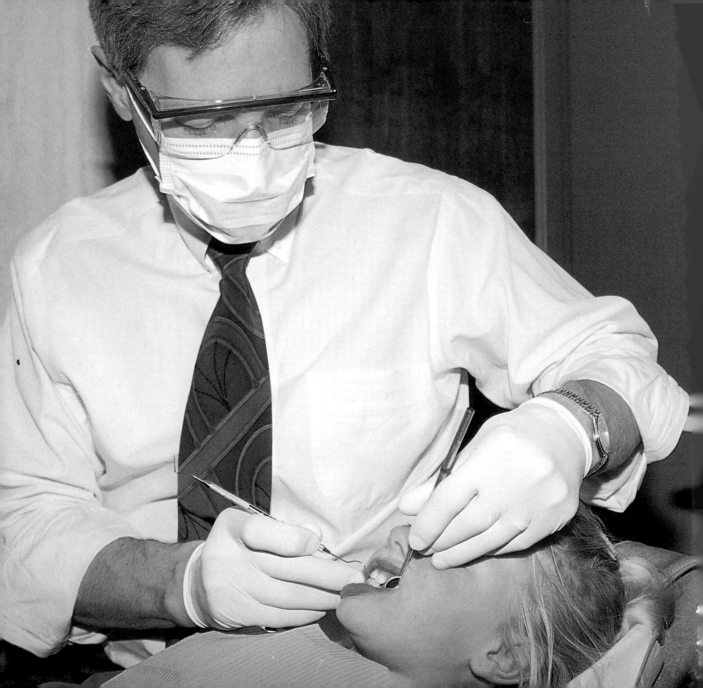

# DENTISTS

Dentists know teeth like rabbits know carrots. Dentists are the tooth experts. When people have problems with their teeth, they find a dentist.

Dentists, though, aren't strictly teeth experts. They also treat problems with the skin, flesh, and bone around teeth.

Dentists are specially trained to identify tooth problems and treat them. They also teach patients with healthy teeth how to keep them that way.

*Dentists fix teeth and show their patients*    5
*how to keep teeth strong and healthy*

# DENTISTRY

The doctor who listens to your heart and tells you to say "aaah" is a doctor of medicine. A dentist is a doctor of dentistry.

Dentistry is both a field of study and a skill. Dentistry deals with the study of problems of teeth and the flesh and bone around them. It also deals with the skills that help dentists discover, treat, and prevent tooth and mouth disease.

*By taking and studying x-ray pictures, a dentist learns about the condition of bone around the teeth*

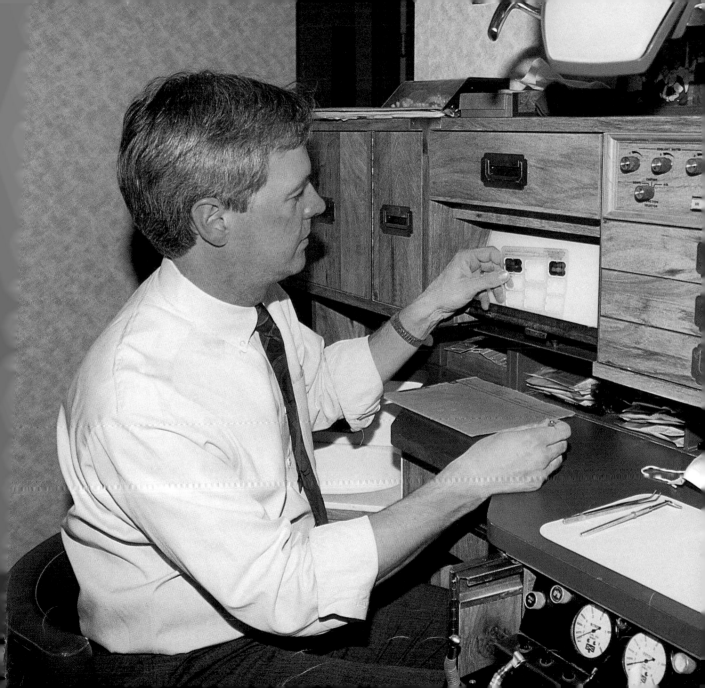

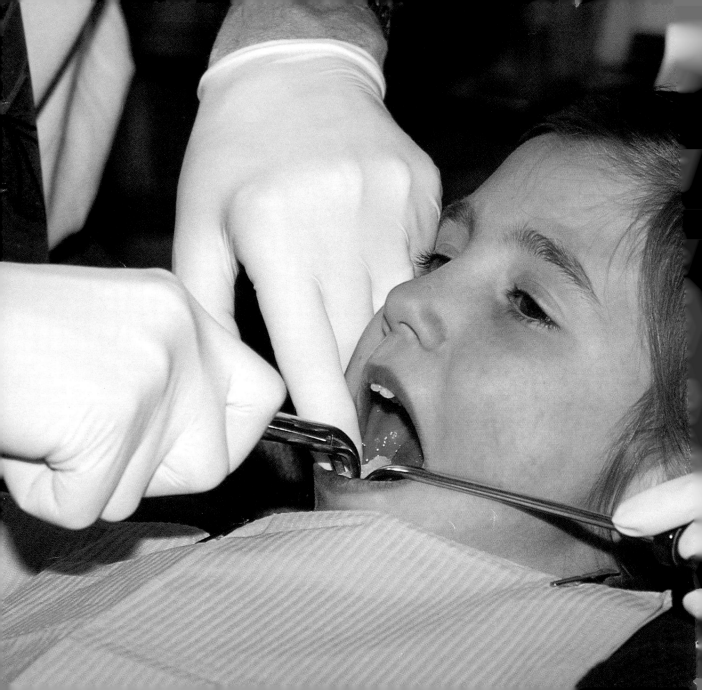

## WHAT DENTISTS DO

Dentists spend a fair amount of job time looking into and working in people's mouths. Dentists examine teeth and sometimes clean and x-ray them.

Dentists have the skills to pull teeth that are causing problems. They fill **cavities** (KAH vih teez) caused by tooth decay. They replace missing teeth with artificial teeth.

Dentists treat mouth infections, attach braces to teeth, and perform many other tasks.

*With a lower forceps, a tooth-pulling instrument, a dentist prepares to remove one of a young patient's baby teeth*

## DENTAL HYGIENE

A dentist and a dentist's helpers show patients how to practice dental **hygiene** (HI jeen). Hygiene is cleanliness. Keeping teeth clean reduces the chance of mouth infection or tooth decay.

A dentist and dental **hygienist** (HI jen ist) teach patients how to brush their teeth properly. They also teach patients to clean the tight spaces between their teeth with threadlike dental **floss** (FLAWSS).

*The dentist's office is a great place to learn dental hygiene and the right way to brush teeth*

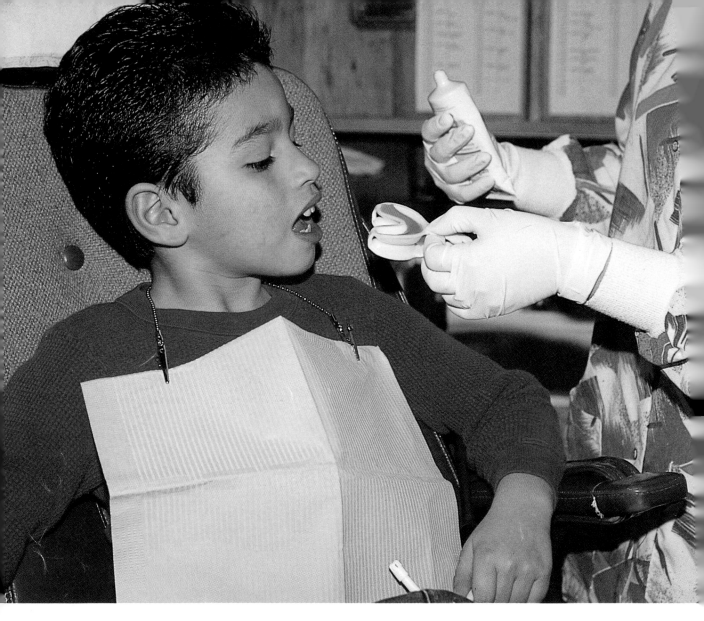

*A patient prepares for a fluoride treatment*

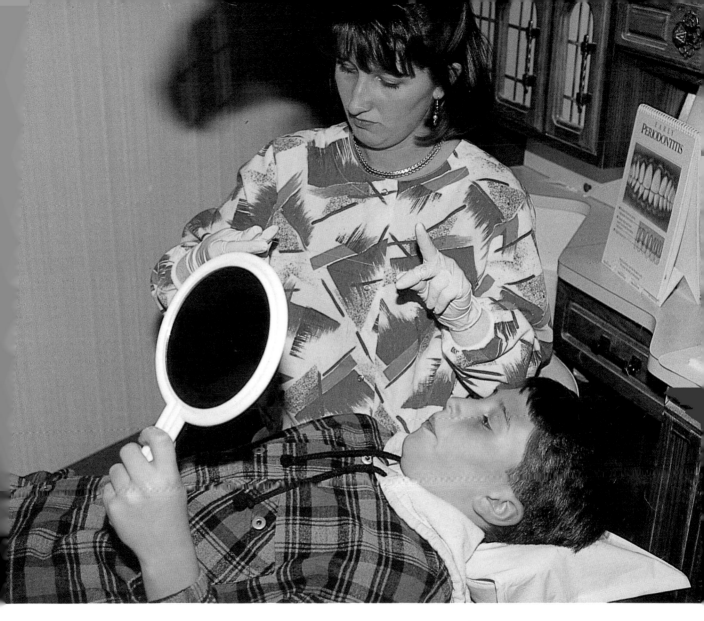

*With a mirror, this patient can watch the dental hygienist floss his teeth*

## KINDS OF DENTISTS

Some dentists treat several different kinds of tooth and mouth problems. These dentists practice "general dentistry."

Dental specialists treat certain special or serious problems. **Oral surgeons** (AW rul SUR jenz), for example, perform **surgery** (SUR jer ee), or operations, on teeth, gums, and jawbones. One group of specialists help force wayward teeth back into proper position with braces.

Other specialists work with such dental problems as gum disease and loss of bone in the jaws.

*A doctor of general dentistry works on filling a patient's cavity*

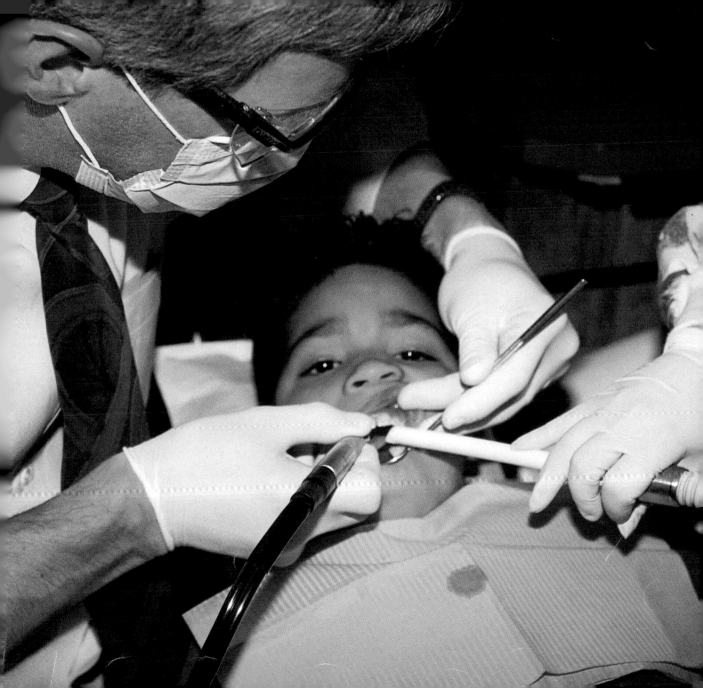

# WHERE DENTISTS WORK

Dentists work in offices where they can treat patients and set up equipment. A dentist may have a single office or a group of offices with a variety of equipment.

Dentists who work together as partners share office space.

Some dentists teach dentistry in colleges and universities or manage schools of dentistry. A few dentists work in large hospitals.

*In a well-equipped dental office, a hygienist prepares a patient for x-rays*

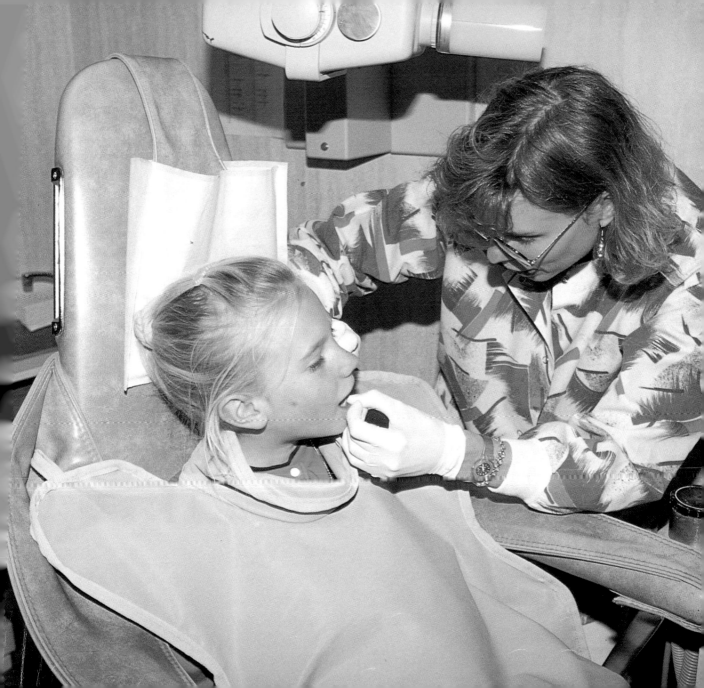

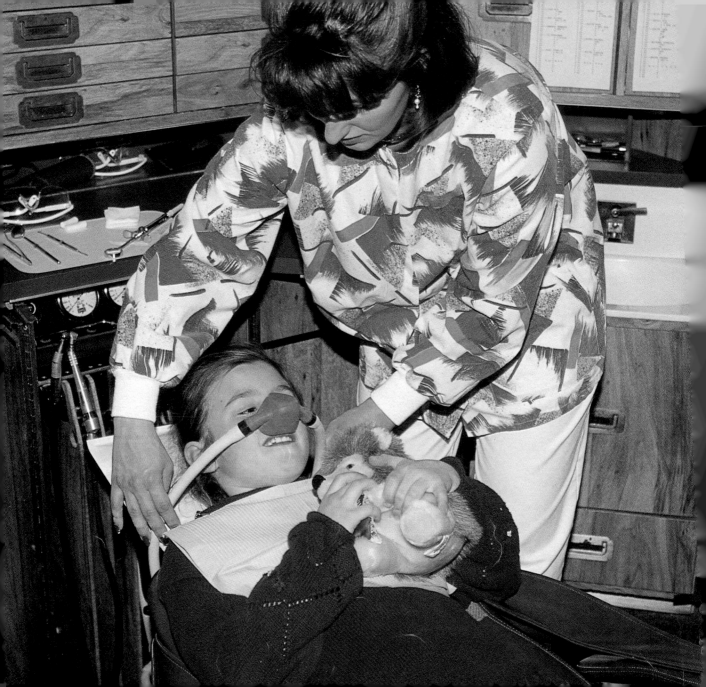

# A DENTIST'S HELPERS

Many dentists hire dental assistants and hygienists. Dental assistants work directly with a dentist. An assistant helps a dentist with such jobs as pulling teeth, filling cavities, and making wax molds of teeth. The molds are used to shape artificial teeth and crowns, or coverings, for natural teeth.

Hygienists take x-rays, carefully clean teeth, and give **fluoride** (FLOOR ide) treatments. Fluoride is a natural substance that helps strengthen teeth.

*A dental assistant prepares a patient for nitrous oxide, or "laughing gas," which will ease the pain of certain dental work*

# A DENTIST'S TOOLS

Dentists use many kinds of instruments, machines, and substances. Dentists use high-speed drills to destroy tooth cavities. They work with filling material of silver, gold, and plastic.

Dentists use sharp metal instruments to clean teeth and cut into gums during operations. They use needles to give drugs that prevent pain in teeth and gums.

Dentists read x-ray pictures from their x-ray machines.

*A facial mask, mirror (right), steel explorer (left), and plastic suction tube (center, in patient's hand) are among several dental tools used in cleaning*

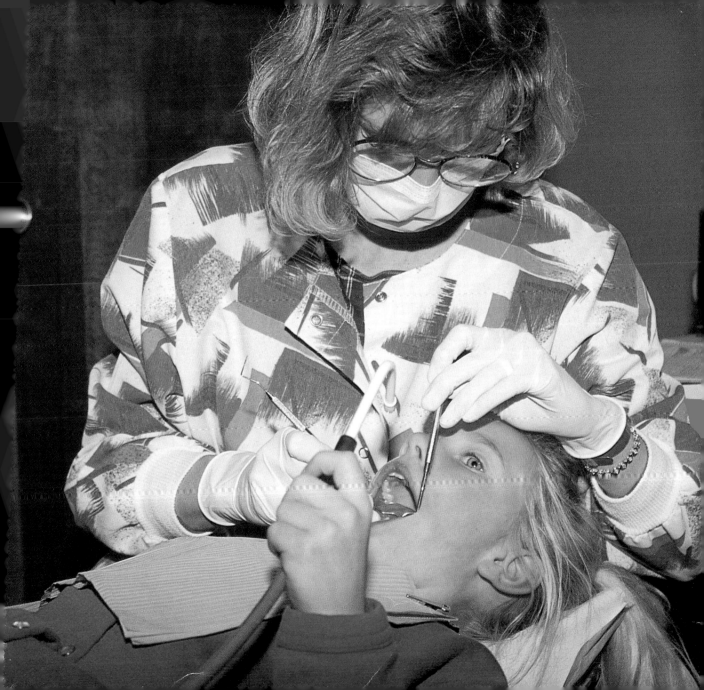

## BECOMING A DENTIST

The path to becoming a dentist is long and difficult. Dentists are highly trained men and women who attend college for about eight years.

A dentist earns a four-year college degree, then attends a dental school. The United States has about 60 dental schools.

Only when a student finishes dental school can he or she be a doctor of dentistry.

## Glossary

**cavity** (KAH vih tee) — in a tooth, a small, hollowed-out place caused by decay

**floss** (FLAWSS) — the string used to clean between teeth; the act of cleaning teeth with floss

**fluoride** (FLOOR ide) — a natural substance found in some water supplies and useful in keeping teeth strong

**hygiene** (HI jeen) — cleanliness for the purpose of good health

**hygienist** (HI jen ihst) — a dentist's assistant who cleans teeth and performs other dental tasks

**oral surgeon** (AW rul SUR jen) — a doctor who performs operations, or surgery, in someone's mouth

**surgery** (SUR jer ee) — a dental operation; a medical act that cuts into some part of the body

# INDEX